Taste Margaret River

Compiled by Kerry Broom

Margaret River

The Margaret River region is one of Western Australia's most popular holiday destinations. A three-and-a-half-hour drive south from Perth, this picturesque locality stretches between Cape Naturaliste and Cape Leeuwin and incorporates the townships of Busselton, Dunsborough, Yallingup, Margaret River and Augusta. These towns overflow each year with visitors seeking to enjoy the most beautiful coastlines, pristine beaches, native bushland, caves, forests, farms, historic sites and the finest gourmet delights from the region's award-winning wineries and first-class restaurants.

Over a century ago, the massive karri and tuart hardwoods that dominated the area were logged in great quantities to supply much needed fuel and building material for urban development throughout Australia and overseas. In the early 1900s the cleared land made way for dairy and beef farming on the rich, rolling pastureland. In the late 1960s the region's soil types and mild coastal climate was found to have much in common with some of the best French wine producing regions and, not surprisingly, winemakers quickly moved to the area to establish their vineyards.

The first vines were planted in 1967, and today Margaret River has a solid reputation as a premium wine grape-growing area. There are now around 80 wineries with approximately 200 vineyards scattered over picture-book hillsides. Many have stylish restaurants and gift galleries, while others provide state-of-the-art tasting facilities, viewing areas and wine tours.

Like the many winemakers who have created some very successful wines, talented chefs have been drawn to the region by the desire to produce dishes with flair and imagination using quality local produce. Delicacies such as oysters, crabs and crayfish, locally farmed marron, rainbow trout, grain-fed beef and freshly harvested fruits and vegetables dominate restaurant menus.

This book showcases the beautiful food and wine available to "taste" in the Margaret River region. It is a celebration of the area's natural beauty, innovative cuisine, world-class wineries and the emergence of a culture that enjoys the best of the good life.

Enjoy!

Restaurants

Thanks to Western Australia's fabulous climate, bountiful seas and fertile soils, an abundance of fresh produce is available throughout the year. In the Margaret River region, there is an impressive variety of restaurants and cafés offering the most tempting seasonal menus created by chefs whose wide-ranging experiences and culinary flair are satisfying the more cosmopolitan appetites – inviting visitors to reap the rewards of this beautiful part of the world.

Along with the restaurants featured in this book we celebrate the special tastes of Margaret River.

Artézen Espresso Bar & Restaurant

Established by Chef Adrian Broom, Artézen is a modern and stylish restaurant centrally located on the main street of Dunsborough. The restaurant and espresso bar boast a beautifully appointed north-facing location where visitors enjoy the morning sun in the centre of town.

The aroma of some of the best coffee in the country and the promise of the most delicious breakfasts and lunches, presented with skill and good humour, welcome guests through the restaurant's doors, which open every day of the week at 7am. The staff play a major role in the restaurant's success as they are bright and accommodating, with highly trained baristas who have a passion for the little black coffee bean. The menu is creative and enticing with local produce gracing the plate daily.

Artézen is a popular place where locals and tourists come to enjoy consistently good food made from the freshest ingredients, and complemented by top quality coffee.

Seared salmon with poached eggs and wilted baby spinach

8 eggs, preferably free-range

40 g butter

4 x 100 g fresh salmon fillets

800 g baby spinach

4 teaspoons lemon juice

4 cloves garlic, crushed (optional)

salt and freshly ground black pepper

4 thick slices sour dough toast

In a shallow saucepan, bring 5 cm of water to the boil. Turn off the heat and add the eggs two at a time directly into the water, carefully opening the two halves of the shells at the water surface so that the eggs slide into the water. This minimises the egg whites spreading.

Cover the pan with a tight-fitting lid. Leave the eggs to cook undisturbed in the water for about three minutes. The eggs are cooked when the whites are opaque. Remove the eggs from the pan with a slotted spoon and drain on a clean tea towel.

Melt the butter in a large frying pan over high heat, add the salmon fillets and sear on each side for one minute, until golden brown. Remove the fillets from the pan and place on a paper towel to drain.

Reduce the heat to medium, add the spinach, lemon juice, garlic, salt and pepper. Toss it together quickly with tongs until the spinach is just wilted.

To serve, top the toast with the spinach, salmon and poached eggs.

(You can make the dish decadent with a hollandaise sauce.)

Serves: four

Lamonts Margaret River

The glinting sunlight reflected on a tranquil lake is the perfect backdrop to enjoy Lamonts Restaurant and cellar door in Yallingup.

Chef and owner Kate Lamont believes that good food can always be found in wine growing regions, so her third restaurant, in the heart of the Margaret River wine region, is certainly true to her philosophy. Lamonts is a pure reflection of Kate's obvious talents and love of good food.

Kate grew up in the Swan Valley of Western Australia among fruit trees and grape vines, learning from an early age the importance of seasonality and fresh quality produce. Kate was born into a winemaking family – her late grandfather, Jack Mann, was highly regarded as a pioneer of WA's wine industry.

Lamonts is a casual, relaxed restaurant with quality food that is delicious and simple, created with the finest ingredients. The wine list is dominated by the family's signature label and is expanded to include other quality vintages.

Crisp-fried marron with cumin salt and lime mayonnaise

Mayonnaise

1 egg yolk

2 tablespoons lime juice

1 teaspoon grated lime zest

salt and freshly ground black pepper

1½ cups robust olive oil

3 teaspoons sea salt

3 teaspoons freshly ground black pepper

3 teaspoons ground cumin

18 small marron, cut in half lengthways, cleaned and patted dry

oil for deep-frying

lime wedges

To make the mayonnaise, in a medium size bowl mix together the egg yolk, lime juice and zest. Season. Gradually whisk in the olive oil – almost drop by drop – until smooth. Add more salt or lime juice if necessary.

For the marron, mix the sea salt, pepper and cumin together in a small pan and dry-fry over medium heat until quite aromatic. Dust the marron with the cumin salt.

Heat the oil in a heavy pan to 170°C and deep-fry the marron halves, a few at a time, until cooked, for about 1-2 minutes.

Serve immediately with the lime mayonnaise and lime wedges on the side, with a glass of chilled semillon sauvignon blanc.

Serves: six

Roasted Margaret River venison with onion purée and truffle oil

1½ kg brown onions, peeled and quartered

50 g salted butter

sea salt

For the marinade:

2 bay leaves

2 cinnamon quills

6 juniper berries

¼ orange, peeled, seeded and roughly chopped

1 brown onion, peeled and roughly chopped

1 carrot, peeled and roughly chopped

1 stick celery, roughly chopped

1 cup (250 ml) red wine

1 cup (250 ml) port

600 g venison backstrap (150g per serve)

20 shallots, peeled with tail left intact

4 bay leaves

2 sprigs thyme

6 black peppercorns

1 litre good quality beef stock

1 red onion, finely sliced

½ cup (125 ml) milk

½ cup (125 g) cornflour

2 cups vegetable oil for deep-frying

truffle oil (available from specialty food shops)

For the onion purée, preheat the oven to 150°C. Put the onions, butter and salt into a deep ovenproof dish, cover and braise until tender, for 4-5 hours. Transfer to a food processor and process until smooth.

To make the marinade, in a mortar, pound together the bay leaves, cinnamon, juniper berries and orange until roughly crushed. Combine with the vegetables, wine and port. Place the venison in a large, sealable container and cover with the marinade. Leave in a cool place to marinate for 1 hour only. Remove the meat from the marinade and set aside. Strain the marinade and reserve the liquid.

To glaze the shallots, combine them with the reserved marinade, the bay leaves, thyme and peppercorns in a heavy pan and heat slowly. Allow the liquid to reduce until the shallots are glazed and tender, about 90 minutes. Remove the shallots and keep warm. Reserve the liquid.

For the beef jus, in a pan over medium heat, combine the stock and reserved glazing liquid, and heat to simmer for 5 minutes.

To cook the meat, preheat the oven to 190°C. Place the venison in a heavy ovenproof pan over medium-high heat. Sear on all sides, turning once. Place the pan in the oven and roast the meat for approximately 5 mins. Cover the meat with foil and leave it to rest for approximately 10 mins.

To make the onion rings, dip the red onion slices in the milk then coat lightly with the cornflour. Heat the oil in a heavy pan on high and drop the onion rings in, a few at a time, to deep-fry until golden. Drain on absorbent paper, keep warm; season to taste.

To serve, reheat the onion purée and shallots in the microwave; place the purée in the middle of each plate and arrange 4-5 shallots around the edge. Slice the venison into 2 pieces per serving and place on top of the purée. Drizzle with the jus and a little truffle oil. Top with 6-8 onion rings.

Serves: four

Wineries

The Margaret River wine region is responsible for only 2% of Australia's total wine production but supplies no less than 20% of the premium wine market. While it has been barely 30 years since the first wines were produced, it is now internationally recognised as one of the most vibrant and exciting wine regions in the world.

Strong soil types and mild coastal conditions combined with sustainable, holistic and environmentally responsible viticulture have enabled the region's winemakers to achieve great results with consistently high-quality fruit.

Forester Estate

Forester Estate is a locally owned winery situated in the northern Margaret River region on Wildwood Road. The property is surrounded by huge eucalypt trees that once supported a thriving timber trade. The estate has a saw pit that was used by the original pioneers to mill timber which was then transported by ox and cart to the nearest railway station. The timber from the property, especially the local hardwood, was shipped from Geographe Bay to countries around the world.

Kevin McKay began winemaking in the vineyards of Margaret River in the early 1980s and purchased the Forester property with his wife Jenny in 2001 where an established vineyard existed. With partners Redmond Sweeny and Michael Landridge, they produce exceptional wines that reflect the premium fruit grown in the Margaret River region, enjoying particular success with their cabernet sauvignon and shiraz wines along with their flavoursome cabernet merlot and chardonnay varieties.

Generations of winemaking coupled with the use of new technology and time will ensure Forester Estate wines achieve complexity and finesse. The Forester style reflects the best possible outcome of the fruit that's grown on the vineyard.

CADUS
03 CHARD
26/3
FORESTER
Estate

FORESTER
Estate
MERLOT
Margaret River
PRODUCT OF AUSTRALIA

Howard Park Wines

Purchased by Jeff and Amy Burch in 1988, Leston Vineyard (named after Jeff's father) is the vine-producing property and home of Howard Park Wines in Margaret River. Jeff and Amy Burch's greatest passions in life include family and wine. The essence of these passions is obvious when discovering Howard Park wines.

At the time of purchase the property was a run-down sheep farm, however the couple succeeded in their ambition to create a showpiece vineyard and state-of-the-art tasting facility incorporating best viticultural practices, with the first planting of vines occurring in 1996.

Howard Park produces riesling, chardonnay, sauvignon blanc, shiraz and cabernet sauvignon from Margaret River and the Great Southern. These are wines of great subtlety, character and elegance and have a proven history of rewarding ageing with increased complexity and interest. The wines, produced in limited quantities, are now exported extensively overseas. Howard Park's reputation of crafting balanced and elegant wines with uncompromising commitment and much pride and passion has become internationally recognised.

Laurance of Margaret River

Laurance Vineyards is a family owned and farmed vineyard located in the Wilyabrup sub-region of Margaret River. Peter and Dianne Laurance fell in love with the property in 2001 with little idea that it would become a successful family business.

The property was originally purchased by the previous owner as grazing land, however it was subsequently identified as a quality viticultural holding. The vines which were planted in 1996 span over 21 hectares with cabernet sauvignon, merlot, shiraz, chardonnay, sauvignon blanc and semillon varieties. They thrive on the fertile soil on this former grazing land which produces fruit rich in intensity, colour and flavour.

The property is exquisite with manicured lawns, a tranquil lake, reflective pond and beautiful perfumed rose gardens, featuring more than 500 rose varieties set under ancient red gums. Bright red azaleas and petunias add an explosion of beauty to the homestead. The state-of-the-art cellar door facility, open in May 2006, is situated in an equally beautiful environment with soft rolling lawns, water features and a gorgeous 1200-bush rose garden.

Located on a truly special property, Laurance of Margaret River offers exceptional and award-winning wines.

PINK

LAURANC
of
MARGARET
WHITE
LAURANCE
of
MARGARET RIVER
RED
LAURANCE
of
MARGARET RIVER
ROSÉ
750ML
AURANCE
AUSTRALIA
MARGARET RIVER
Just a Sweetie
350ML

Palmer Wines

Established by Stephen and Helen Palmer in 1977 as one of the pioneer vineyards in the Margaret River region, the initial plantings on the banks of the fertile Wilyabrup River included chardonnay, semillon, sauvignon blanc and a small amount of cabernet sauvignon and merlot. Hard work and creative winemaking soon paid dividends, and Palmer Wines collected many awards, building an enviable reputation. In the late 1980s a second property was acquired. Located higher up the valley and focusing on high-quality red wine, the "Golden Ponds" property has been another success, with a showpiece being their 1999 Shiraz.

Palmer Wines sell predominantly to international private clients by mail order, with select leading Australian restaurants purchasing the balance of their wines. In 2003 winemaker Bruce Dukes joined the Palmer Wines team with an aim to excel in producing the ultimate in wine to be enjoyed by epicureans from around the world.

QANTAS WINE SHOW OF WESTERN AUSTRALIA
GOLD MEDAL
Mt. Barker 2004
PALMER
2005
Sauvignon
Blanc
RIVER

Winery Restaurants

The Margaret River wine region is home to around 200 vineyards and 80 wineries, many of which have established modern restaurants and cellar door facilities that allow visitors to delight in this world-renowned food and wine culture.

Talented winemakers are producing award-winning wines with distinctive flavours and international appeal, and high-calibre chefs are creating exquisite dishes that marry perfectly with the wines – showcasing the beauty and uniqueness this region has to offer.

Clairault Wines

The picturesque Clairault property at the head of Gunyulgup Creek was purchased in 1999 by Bill and Edna Martin. It boasts an exquisite setting with the winery, restaurant and tasting areas blending seamlessly to allow visitors to enjoy some of the finest wine and food in the region.

Clairault is a family-run business under the expert direction of Conor Martin. Their passion for creating quality wines is well established in Australia and they are a major player in the international arena.

Clairault winery is one of the oldest in the region and offers a range of estate wines as well as a selection of rare museum releases, including a number of award-winning wines, each showing exceptional balance, structure and individuality.

The pairing of superb produce-focused dishes with their wines is a driving force behind the popularity and reputation of Clairault Wines. The food is a visual feast and taste sensation.

Clairault's continual achievement of excellence has been highlighted with the restaurant receiving the acclaimed Black Star rating by Australia's Gourmet Traveller 2005 Best Restaurant Guide.

Clairault is an impressive high-profile winery and restaurant in a truly unique location.

Red duck curry

400 ml (2 tins) coconut milk

4 tablespoons Thai red curry paste

4 duck Marylands (the whole leg including the thigh), each cut into 5-6 pieces on the bone

3 tablespoons fish sauce

2 tablespoons palm sugar

juice of 1 lime

1 cup water

2 red chillies, thinly sliced diagonally

6-8 Kaffir lime leaves, finely sliced

6 shallots, peeled and halved

8 lychees, halved

½ cup Thai basil, torn

In a wide saucepan on high, heat the curry paste in a little of the coconut milk until aromatic, for about 2 minutes. Reduce the heat, add the rest of the milk and the duck pieces and simmer for a few minutes. Add the fish sauce, sugar, lime juice, water, chillies, lime leaves and shallots and simmer until the meat is tender, about 45 minutes.

Add the lychees. Check the seasoning and add extra fish sauce if required. Add the basil and garnish with a sprig of coriander and lime leaves, if desired. Serve with jasmine rice.

Serves: four

Recommended wine: Clairault Cape Pink 2005

Leeuwin Estate

The Leeuwin Estate Winery and Restaurant is located on 275 acres of immaculately tendered land and is one of the showpieces of the region. The property was a cattle farm when the Horgan family set out with the vision to transform it into one of Australia's most successful wine producers.

Today, tens of thousands of visitors, from discerning wine connoisseurs to tourists from around the world, come each year not only to enjoy the estate's outstanding wines but to also experience the award-winning restaurant and tourist facility, most notably its glorious grassed amphitheatre. The food is adventurous and carefully considered, incorporating contrast in texture, neatly balanced flavours and beautiful presentation.

Every summer this magnificent venue is the setting for sell-out concerts when the vineyard comes alive to the wonderful sounds of some of the world's greatest musicians. This unique bushland setting, framed by majestic karri trees, is also the perfect backdrop to enjoy a picnic and taste the superb Leeuwin Estate wines which rank alongside the world's finest.

Saffron roasted salmon with asparagus and artichoke salad

pinch of saffron

250 ml extra virgin olive oil

zest of two lemons

1 fennel bulb, outer shell trimmed off, leaves chopped

4 x 170 g salmon fillets, scaled, skin intact

sea salt and freshly ground pepper

125 g butter

4-6 Jerusalem artichokes, peeled and sliced (leave in water with lemon juice to prevent browning)

8 spears Vasse asparagus, sliced thinly

1 cup watercress, picked and washed

100 ml fish stock

To make the saffron oil, in a small pan moisten the saffron with 30 ml water. Bring to the boil and reduce the liquid until nearly dry. Add 100 ml olive oil and cook over medium heat for 10 minutes. Allow to cool. To make the lemon oil, slowly heat half the lemon zest in 100 ml olive oil to reach a simmer. Cool and strain. Set aside.

Preheat oven to 150°C, coat the fennel bulb with the remaining olive oil and place in an ovenproof dish. Slowly cook for 2 hours. Remove from the oven and leave to cool; drain, then finely slice.

In a pot, cover the remaining zest with water and bring to the boil. Drain and refresh in cold water. Repeat this process three times to remove bitter citric acid. Add the sliced fennel and fennel leaves. Set aside.

Season the salmon with sea salt and pepper then cook the fillets over a hot grill, skin side down, until crisp. Turn over and seal the flesh side. Transfer to a roasting tray, skin side up, brush with ample saffron oil and a knob of butter on top, and roast in a preheated 180°C oven for about 8-10 minutes until firm, then let rest for 6 minutes before serving.

To make the salad, boil the artichoke slices in a pot of salted water until soft; remove with a slotted spoon. Blanch the asparagus in the boiling water for 10 seconds; refresh under cold water; drain. In a stainless steel bowl combine the artichoke, asparagus and watercress. Drizzle with some of the lemon oil and stock dressing.

To serve, warm the lemon fennel confit and place in the centre of each plate. Place the salmon on the fennel and pour over some of the cooking juices. Garnish with the salad and drizzle over the remaining dressing.

Serves: four

Recommended wine: Leeuwin Estate Art Series Chardonnay

Damara lamb rack with celeriac caponata and salsa dragoncello

Lamb Sauce

1 kg lamb bones, chopped

1 carrot, peeled and chopped

1 leek, washed and chopped

2 onions, peeled and chopped

1 clove garlic, crushed

1 sprig thyme

2 tomatoes, deseeded and chopped

1 tablespoon tomato paste

1 cup red wine

1 litre good-quality veal or beef stock

Caponata

150 g caster sugar

1 tablespoon water

125 ml red wine vinegar

1 bay leaf

3 cloves garlic, crushed

½ large eggplant, cut into 2-cm cubes

salt and black pepper

1 tablespoon extra virgin olive oil

1 celeriac, peeled and diced

125 g celery heart, cut into 1-cm dices

50 g pine nuts, roasted

5 roma tomatoes, peeled, deseeded and cut into 1-cm cubes

1 small bunch basil, picked and washed

Salsa Dragoncello

150 g stale sour dough bread, crusts removed

4 cloves garlic

20 g salt

1 cup tarragon leaves, picked, washed and dried

100 ml red wine vinegar

150 ml extra virgin olive oil

4 Damara 5-point lamb racks

To make the sauce, roast the lamb bones in a preheated 180°C oven until brown, for about 30 minutes. Drain off the fat, reserving 1-2 tablespoons. Place the carrot, leek, onions and reserved fat in a pot and sauté over medium heat until soft and caramelised. Add the garlic, herbs, tomatoes and tomato paste and cook until the mixture reaches a jam consistency. Deglaze the pan with the wine, cooking until the liquid has reduced back to a jam. Add the bones and the stock and slowly bring to a boil, skimming off any fat that comes to the surface. Reduce the heat and simmer until it reaches a sauce consistency. Allow to cool, then finely strain the liquid again.

To make the caponata, combine the sugar and water in pan over medium heat and cook until caramelised (golden). Reduce the heat, add the vinegar, bay leaf and garlic and cook until syrupy. Season with salt. Coat the eggplant in salt and place in a colander for 30 minutes. Rinse in water and drain well. Heat the olive oil in a frying pan and sauté the eggplant until softened and golden. Remove with a slotted spoon and drain on absorbent paper. Return the pan to the heat and cook the celeriac over low heat until soft. Blanch the celery in a pot of boiling salted water. Refresh under cold water; drain. Combine all the vegetables with the pine nuts and heat through with the syrup. Remove from the heat and add the basil to wilt. Set aside.

To make the dragoncello, in a food processor, blend the bread, garlic, salt and herbs, and gradually add the vinegar and olive oil until well mixed.

Preheat the oven to 150°C. Lightly season the lamb and fry in a hot ovenproof pan to seal each side, turning once. Place in the oven and slowly roast to medium rare, about 15 minutes. Loosely cover with foil and allow to rest before carving.

To serve, place the lamb rack on a bed of warmed caponata with salsa dragoncello on the side. Glaze with warm lamb sauce.

Serves: four

Recommended wine: Leeuwin Estate 2003 Art Series Shiraz

Voyager Estate

Just south of Margaret River on Stevens Road is one of the most striking estates in the region. Inspired by Cape Dutch architecture, the restaurant building features white rendered finishes and elegant gables surrounded by beautiful formal gardens full of roses, lavender and gardenias – a reminder that the first vine cuttings were introduced to Western Australia from South Africa in 1829.

Proprietor Michael Wright and his team produce a select range of very successful handcrafted premium wines highlighting the exceptional regional characters that give Margaret River its prestigious reputation. The winery combines art and science to develop the fruit into wines distinguished by their purity, finesse, structure and balance.

In 2005 Voyager Estate won two Gold Plate Awards for "Restaurant within a Winery" and "Tourist Restaurant: Country". A stylishly decorated hallway leads to a formal dining area where antique tables and gracious furnishings create a warm and welcoming environment. The focus is on inventive, modern Australian cuisine driven by fresh produce, with each dish being expertly matched with Voyager's award-winning selection of current and museum release wines.

Soft-baked mozzarella tartlet

1 small jar (about 250 g) blood orange marmalade

100 ml orange juice

For the pesto

¾ cup basil leaves, firmly packed

30 g pine nuts

20 g parmesan cheese

50 ml olive oil

1 clove garlic, peeled

2 sheets puff pastry

1 egg

30 ml milk

6 buffalo-milk tomato size mozzarella, or 2 lime-size bocconcini (available from specialty food shops), each sliced into three pieces

2 pears, thinly sliced

50 g pistachio nuts, roughly chopped

1 small bunch *tatsoi* (or baby spinach leaves or rocket), washed and dried

Place the marmalade in a saucepan with the orange juice and cook over medium heat until it reaches a syrupy consistency. Pass through a sieve and set the syrup aside.

To make the pesto, place the basil, pine nuts, parmesan , olive oil and garlic in a food processor and blend until smooth. Add a touch more oil if too chunky. Season to taste. Set aside.

Cut out six 10-cm discs of pastry and place them on a baking tray. Beat the egg and milk together and brush the mixture over the pastry. Cook in a preheated 180°C oven for about 5-6 minutes or until golden brown. Remove from the oven and let cool slightly.

Smear each piece of pastry with a tablespoon of pesto and top with 3 pieces of mozzarella. Bake until the mozzarella starts to melt.

In a bowl toss the pear slices with the *tatsoi,* half of the pistachio nuts and a squirt of the orange syrup. Mix well.

To serve, place each mozzarella tart in the centre of a plate and sprinkle the rest of the pistachio nuts around. Top with a good handful of the pear salad, drizzled with the remaining syrup.

Serves: six

Recommended wine: Voyager Estate 2004 Chardonnay

Chocolate tart

Pastry

125 g unsalted butter

125 g caster sugar

1 teaspoon vanilla essence

150 g plain flour

50 g cocoa powder

Filling

525 ml pouring cream

715 g good-quality dark, bittersweet cooking chocolate

To make the pastry, cream the butter and sugar in a electric mixer until pale, then mix in the vanilla essence. Sift the flour and cocoa powder together and incorporate into the butter mixture until a wet dough has formed.

Grease a 24-cm fluted flan tin, preferably one with a removable base, and press the dough into the sides and over the base, ensuring the pastry is evenly distributed. Rest the pastry in the refrigerator for 1 hour.

Preheat oven to180°C and bake the pastry for 10 minutes. The pastry will bubble up slightly and the sides may shrink a little, so after it is cooked and while it is still hot and malleable, quickly press the pastry back into its original shape using a clean tea towel.

To make the filling, shave the chocolate into a large mixing bowl and set aside. Bring the cream to simmering point in a saucepan over medium heat. Pour the cream over the chocolate, stirring until combined. Pour the mixture into the hot tart shell without delay.

Refrigerate immediately, on a flat surface, and leave for at least 4 hours to set.

Serves: ten

Recommended wine: Voyager Cabernet Sauvignon Merlot

Watershed Premium Wines

Beyond an imposing stone-wall entrance is an impressive panoramic view over the magnificent dam and expansive Watershed vineyard. The beautifully appointed wine tasting facility and restaurant offer numerous award-winning wines including cabernet sauvignon, merlot, shiraz, chardonnay and sauvignon blanc premium wines. The location is ideal – bounded by the cool southern touch of the Indian Ocean and blessed with a Mediterranean climate. Watershed produces wines that have a distinctive elegance and power, with complex fruit flavours and intense bouquets.

The restaurant menu features a wide range of innovative and flavoursome dishes, highlighting seafood and local produce such as venison, and a selection of Margaret River cheeses.

Watershed is a unique dining experience catering for the whole family and those who enjoy good food and wine at reasonable prices.

Tempura dhufish rolls with seared scallops and green papaya salad

Caramel

250 g caster sugar

250 ml water

1 stick lemon grass

1 green chilli, halved lengthwise

1 cinnamon stick

1 pod star anise

100 ml fish sauce

100 ml rice wine vinegar

300 ml fresh orange juice, strained

Salad

¼ papaya, peeled, deseeded and julienned

1 large red chilli, deseeded, flesh removed and julienned

2 sticks spring onions, julienned

100 g *wakami* salad (available from specialty food shops)

1 tablespoon onion seeds

lemon oil for dressing (see p 37)

Tempura rolls

2 large green chillies

4 cloves garlic

½ cup coriander leaves

1 stick of lemon grass

¼ cup Vietnamese mint

500g dhufish flesh

2 large eggs (whites only)

30 ml fish sauce

salt and pepper

4 *nori* sheets

300 g tempura batter (available from specialty food shops)

200 g flour

500 ml soda water

vegetable oil for deep-frying

12 scallops

For the caramel, put the sugar, water, lemon grass, chilli, cinnamon and star anise in a pot with a sugar thermometer and bring to the boil over medium heat until it reaches 140°C (or just before it starts to colour or caramelise).

Remove from heat, let cool slightly, then add the fish sauce, rice wine vinegar, and juice. Strain out the solids just before serving.

To prepare the salad, place the papaya, chilli and onions in a small bowl with the *wakami*, onion seeds and lemon oil. Toss gently.

To make the tempura rolls, place the chillies, garlic, coriander, lemon grass and mint in a food processor and purée until quite fine (but not a paste). Add the fish and continue to process until combined. Add the egg whites, fish sauce and seasoning, and mix until smooth.

Using a piping bag with a large nozzle pipe, squeeze the fish mixture onto the centre of each *nori* sheet. Using a pastry brush dipped into water, moisten the edges of the sheets, then roll them up around the fish mixture, into a cigar-like shape.

In a mixing bowl, whisk the tempura batter into the soda water. Heat the oil in a heavy pan slowly over medium heat until hot enough to fry. If a little batter dropped into the oil rises to the top, then the oil is ready. Dust each roll lightly with flour, dip into the batter and drop gently into the oil to fry until golden.

Sear the scallops individually on a barbecue grill for 1½ minutes on each side, turning once.

Serve the tempura rolls, cut in half, with the scallops topped with a small amount of salad and orange caramel in a small dipping bowl on the side.

Serves: four

Recommended wine: Watershed 2005 Sauvignon Blanc Semillon

Pineapple parfait with blood orange and coconut sorbet

½ Bethonga pineapple, skinned and chopped

¼ vanilla pod, split, seeded

100 g water

150 g caster sugar

4 egg yolks, whipped until light and fluffy

250 ml cream, whipped

350 g blood orange, puréed and strained

100 ml coconut milk

60 g liquid glucose

Nougat (this can also be purchased)

125 g caster sugar

80 g honey

50 g liquid glucose

70 ml water

2 large eggs, whites only, beaten until stiff

¼ teaspoon vanilla extract

200 g Brazil nuts

Fruit wafers

100 g sugar

100 ml water

1 blood orange, cut into 1-mm discs

praline for the garnish (available from specialty food shops)

To make the parfait, place half the pineapple in a food processor with the vanilla and purée for 4 minutes on high; set aside. In a pot over medium heat, and using a sugar thermometer, bring the water and 100 g of the sugar to the boil. When the temperature reaches 138°C (just before the mixture colours), remove the pot from the stove. Pour the sugar mixture slowly onto the yolks and whip until the mixture is cool. Add the pineapple purée. Fold the mixture into the whipped cream, pour into 6 moulds (or cups) and freeze overnight.

To make the sorbet, place the orange purée, the remaining 50 g of the sugar, coconut milk and glucose in a food processor and purée together until smooth. Place in a 500 ml container, cover and freeze overnight.

To make the nougat, place the sugar, honey, glucose and water in pot with a sugar thermometer and bring to the boil. When it reaches 140°C remove from the heat and pour slowly over the stiff egg whites, beating continuously. Stir in the vanilla and nuts. Spoon the mixture into a cake tin lined with rice paper. Spread out evenly then cover with another layer of rice paper. Place a weight on top, then cover and leave at room temperature overnight to set. When set, cut into small sticks using a sharp knife.

To make the wafers, place the sugar and water in pot and boil for 8 minutes, or until the sugar looks as though it has thickened. Remove from the stove and allow to cool slightly.

Slice the remaining pineapple into 1-mm discs and place in a bowl with the orange slices. Pour the liquid over, and allow to cool for 5-10 minutes. Pick up one piece of fruit at a time, allowing the liquid to drain off, and place individually on a tray lined with baking paper. Place in a preheated 80°C oven for 4 hours, then remove and allow to cool. When cool, peel the paper from the wafers.

To serve, unmould the parfaits in the centre of each plate, surround with a few pieces of nougat and top with pineapple wafers, a scoop of sorbet and the orange wafers. Garnish with crumbled praline, if desired.

Serves: six

Recommended wine: Watershed 2005 Viognier

Wills Domain

With a modern yet warm and welcoming design, Wills Domain cellar door opened at the start of 2005 and boasts a stunning view over the rolling hills of Yallingup. High above the Indian Ocean with jarrah and marri trees nurturing red gravel soils on steep sun-drenched western facing slopes the property forms a wine terroir that will become the envy of the industry.

Margaret River's Haunold family, father-to-son vignerons since 1383, were bestowed land and titles in Austria for viticultural excellence over 600 years ago.

Darren Haunold and his family built this beautiful facility with a belief that winemaking is an art form, an artistic impression, where the grapes are lovingly fashioned from the vine by hand. Darren's approach paid off when he won the 2004 WA Wine Industry Young Achiever Award, and their celebrated semillon sauvignon blanc is considered one of the best in Australia.

In addition to their impressive wine list, Wills Domain offer a delicious selection of local food including taste plates and cheese boards that are carefully prepared to complement their beautiful wines. The following recipe is a family favourite.

Lamb shanks

¼ cup plain flour

salt and freshly ground black pepper

6 lamb shanks

50 ml olive oil

2 large onions, diced

1 head of garlic, all cloves peeled and left whole

1 parsnip, diced

2 carrots, diced

2 celery stalks, chopped

3 tablespoons tomato paste

2 teaspoon sweet paprika

250 ml red wine

250 ml beef, lamb or chicken stock

Gremolata

1 large garlic clove, peeled and diced

1 handful flat-leaved parsley, finely chopped

zest of 1 lemon

Dust the lamb shanks with the seasoned flour. Heat the olive oil in a heavy based pan and sauté the shanks, turning them often, until they are brown. Set them aside. In the same pan (adding a little more olive oil if necessary), gently cook the onions and garlic cloves until the onions are soft and translucent. Add the rest of the vegetables, the tomato paste and the paprika. Cook over medium heat for about ten minutes, stirring occasionally. Turn the heat to high, add the wine and stock and bring to a simmer.

Place the shanks in a large casserole dish and cover them well with the vegetable mixture. Seal the dish with a lid and cook in a preheated 100-120°C oven for 3-4 hours until very tender.

To make the gremolata, combine all the ingredients in a bowl. Stir it through the lamb shanks with a little scattered on top, before serving with mashed potatoes or rice.

Serves: six

Recommended wine: Wills Domain Cabernet Sauvignon

Wise Winery & Vineyard Restaurant

Wise Winery was established in 1991 by Ron and Sandra Wise and boasts a breathtaking view sweeping 180 degrees over the lush, green valley of vines and natural bush to the expanse of Geographe Bay. The boutique vineyard showcases top quality vines with sauvignon blanc, semillon, merlot and shiraz plantings presenting excellent fruit for Ron's team of winemakers who consistently produce a first-class range of premium wines.

The Wise Winery & Vineyard Restaurant is owned and operated by chef Heath Townsend who has developed Wise into a stylish yet relaxed premises committed to utilising the finest fresh local produce. City-smart food is combined with casual dining, ensuring travellers and locals who flock to this beautiful setting will be rewarded with continued excellence.

Wise Winery & Vineyard Restaurant is a four-time finalist in the prestigious Gold Plate Awards and is regularly included in Gourmet Traveller's Guide to the Best Restaurants in Australia.

Complemented by a magnificent location, the Wise Winery & Vineyard Restaurant has established itself as one of the most popular in the region.

Local dhufish with cherry tomatoes, olives and thyme

150 ml extra virgin olive oil

10 cloves garlic

1 punnet cherry tomatoes

125 g black olives, pitted

1 bunch of fresh thyme

4 x 170 g dhufish fillets

2 fresh limes, quartered

flat-leaved parsley

salt and freshly ground pepper

In a small pan, heat most of the olive oil with the garlic until it simmers. Remove the pan from the heat and add the tomatoes, olives and thyme. Set aside to infuse for 30 mins.

Heat the remaining olive oil in a frying pan over medium heat. Season the oil then add the dhufish fillets and cook for about 4 minutes. Turn the fish over and cook for a further 3 minutes or until cooked.

To serve, spoon the cherry tomato mix onto 4 warm plates and top with the dhufish. Garnish with parsley and lime wedges on the side.

Serves: four

Recommended wine: Wise Single Vineyard Chardonnay

Blue manna crab with spaghettini

1 brown onion, finely chopped

3 cloves garlic, crushed

10 basil leaves, chopped

100 ml extra virgin olive oil

2 x 440 g tins whole peeled tomatoes

4 cloves garlic, peeled and finely sliced

400 g fresh blue manna crab meat

500 g spaghettini

salt and freshly ground pepper

Sauté the onion, crushed garlic and basil in half the olive oil over medium heat for 1-2 minutes. Add the tomatoes and bring the liquid to a boil. Reduce the heat and simmer for approximately 30 minutes. Transfer to a food processor and purée until smooth. Season to taste.

In a large frying pan over medium heat sauté the sliced garlic in the remaining olive oil until it starts to colour. Add the crab meat and sauté quickly. Season to taste. Spoon in the tomato mixture and cook to reduce the liquid slightly.

Cook the spaghettini in a large pot of salted boiling water until *al dente*. Drain and add to the crab mix.

To serve, divide the spaghettini evenly between 4 serving bowls and drizzle with a little oil. Garnish with some shredded basil and lemon wedges, if desired.

Serves: four

Recommended wine: Wise Unwooded Chardonnay

48213

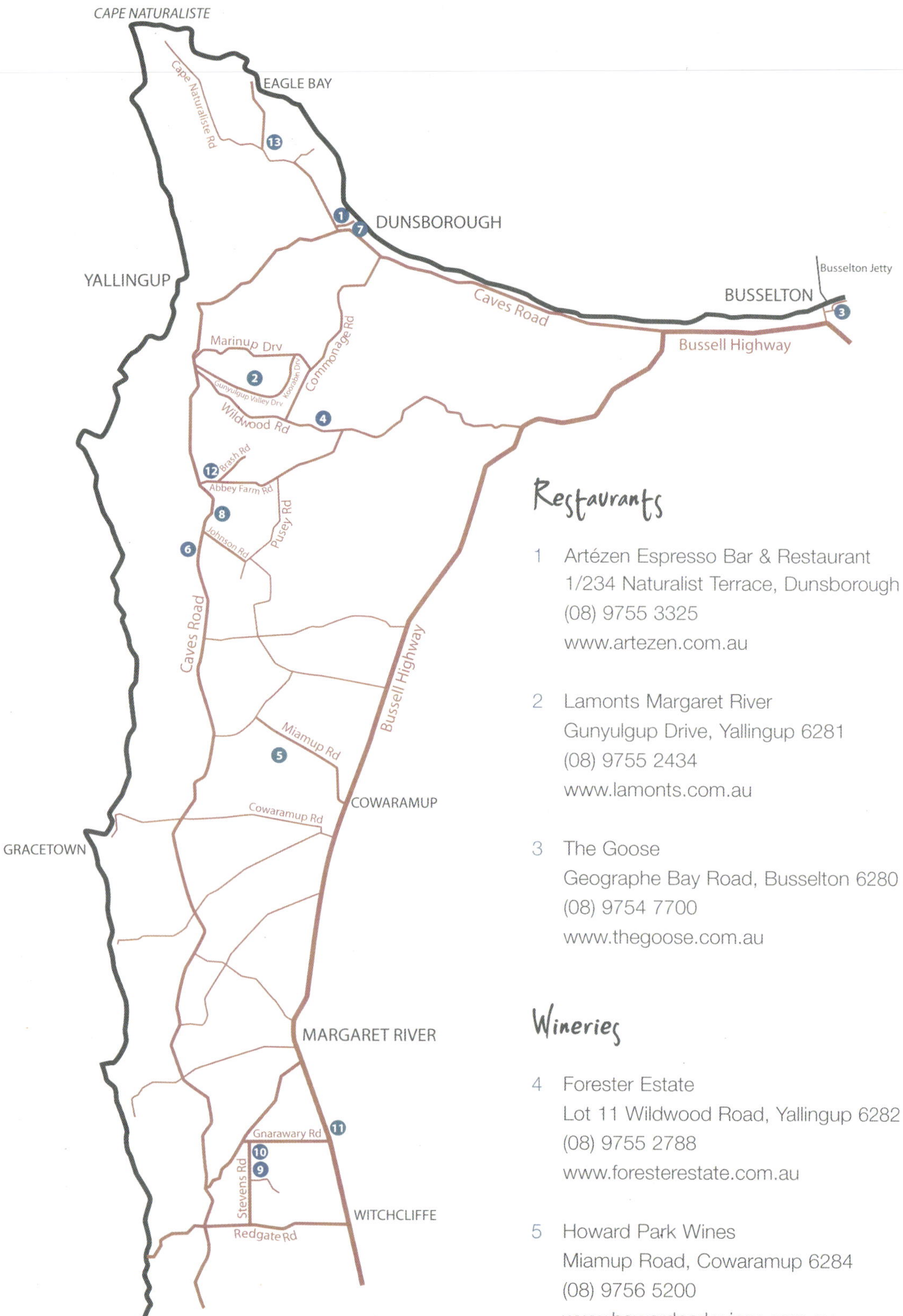

Restaurants

1 Artézen Espresso Bar & Restaurant
1/234 Naturalist Terrace, Dunsborough 6281
(08) 9755 3325
www.artezen.com.au

2 Lamonts Margaret River
Gunyulgup Drive, Yallingup 6281
(08) 9755 2434
www.lamonts.com.au

3 The Goose
Geographe Bay Road, Busselton 6280
(08) 9754 7700
www.thegoose.com.au

Wineries

4 Forester Estate
Lot 11 Wildwood Road, Yallingup 6282
(08) 9755 2788
www.foresterestate.com.au

5 Howard Park Wines
Miamup Road, Cowaramup 6284
(08) 9756 5200
www.howardparkwines.com.au

6 Laurance of Margaret River
Lot 549 Caves Road, Wilyabrup 6280
(08) 9321 8015
www.laurancewines.com.au

7 Palmer Wines
29 Dunn Bay Road, Dunsborough 2681
(08) 9756 7388

Winery Restaurants

8 Clairault Wines
Caves Road, Wilyabrup 6280
(08) 9755 6225
www.clairaultwines.com.au

9 Leeuwin Estate
Stevens Road, Margaret River 6285
(08) 9759 0000
www.leeuwinestate.com.au

10 Voyager Estate
Stevens Road, Margaret River 6285
(08) 9757 6354
www.voyagerestate.com.au

11 Watershed Premium Wines
Bussell Highway, Margaret River 6285
(08) 9758 8633
www.watershedwines.com.au

12 Wills Domain
Brash Road (Cnr Abbey Farm Road),
Yallingup 6282
(08) 9755 2172
www.willsdomain.com.au

13 Wise Winery & Vineyard Restaurant
80 Eagle Bay Road, Dunsborough 6281
(08) 9755 3331
www.wisewine.com.au